EXTREME SPORTS BIOGRAPHIES™

DAVE MIRRA

BMX SUPERSTAR

AARON ROSENBERG

The Rosen Publishing Group, Inc., New York

To Rachel, another Greenville gem

Published in 2005 by The Rosen Publishing Group, Inc.
29 East 21st Street, New York, NY 10010

First Edition

Library of Congress Cataloging-in-Publication Data

Rosenberg, Aaron.
Dave Mirra / by Aaron Rosenberg.— 1st ed.
    p. cm. — (Extreme sports biographies)
Summary: Profiles Dave Mirra, a native New Yorker and a bicycle motocross champion, focusing on the tricks and stunts he performs at the X-Games and other competitions.
Includes bibliographical references and index.
ISBN 1-4042-0067-3 (library binding)
1. Mirra, Dave, 1974– —Juvenile literature. 2. Cyclists—United States—Biography—Juvenile literature. 3. Bicycle motocross—Juvenile literature. [1. Mirra, Dave, 1974– 2. Bicyclists. 3. Bicycle motocross.]
I. Title. II. Series: Extreme sports biographies (Rosen Publishing Group)
GV1051.M57R67 2004
796.6'2'092–dc22
                                                    2003022259

Manufactured in the United States of America

On the cover: Left: Dave Mirra competing in San Francisco, California. Right: Dave Mirra.

CONTENTS

Some athletes have fought uphill battles, trying to get their athletic activities recognized as legitimate sports. Others have had less difficulty, quickly grabbing attention around the nation. Bicyclists have had, perhaps, the easiest time of it. People have been riding bikes for almost two centuries. Baron Karl de Drais de Sauerbrun of Germany is credited with creating the first bike, a *draisienne*, back in 1817. However, the idea of a bike with pedals did not occur until the velocipede in the 1860s. Most people rode their bikes on level surfaces and paved roads, but some bikers had the idea of playing around a little.

In the early 1970s, a group of bike enthusiasts, known as the Klunkers, began modifying "clunky" old bikes for off-road use. This soon caught on, and ever since, people have been doing tricks and stunts on their bikes, riding them over challenging terrain, and generally competing to be the fastest, the most daring, and the best. It's not surprising, then, that most people had no problem recognizing this style of biking as a sport and off-road biking, or BMX, as an extreme sport. It's no surprise, either, that, since biking is one of the two most widely recognized and respected extreme sports (the other being

The sport of off-road biking, or BMX, has come a long way since it first appeared in the 1970s. Superstars like Dave Mirra *(opposite)* have helped increase the sport's popularity.

Baron Karl de Drais de Sauerbrun invented the precursor to the bicycle in Paris in 1817. On a draisienne, the rider propelled himself or herself along by paddling his or her feet against the ground. The modern-day bicycle (complete with pedals) was first produced in 1862 and was known as the velocipede.

skateboarding), its champions are also well known and very popular. And one of the biggest stars in the world of BMX is Dave Mirra.

Dave has been biking professionally for almost a decade now and is still one of the most successful athletes in the sport—he holds more X Games gold medals than any other X Games competitor. His success can also be attributed to his approach both to the sport and to its fans. In many ways, Dave has demonstrated that he has what it takes to be a real star.

His success comes not just from his biking ability but also from his personality. Dave has consistently fostered his relationship with his fans and continues to inspire future generations of BMX stars. His popularity has translated into endorsements, video games, and other areas that have turned Dave into a superstar in his sport. Much like BMX and extreme sports in general, there seems to be no limit to Dave Mirra's popularity.

CHAPTER ONE
BEGINNINGS

David Michael Mirra was born on April 4, 1974, in Syracuse, New York, to Mike and Linda Mirra. Dave learned to ride a bike at the age of four. He and his older brother, Tim, were friends with several other kids in the neighborhood, including some older kids who were already into bikes and could do some basic stunts. Dave and his friends would ride whenever they had the chance and started doing stunts almost immediately.

By the time he was five, Dave was jumping curbs and sailing over handmade dirt ramps. He, his brother,

A rider gets air in Southern California, the birthplace of the modern BMX movement. Dirt jumping is the oldest form of BMX.

and their cousin would ride together every day after school. Jumping curbs and popping wheelies were standard fare. But rather than racing their bikes, Dave and the others worked on impressing one another with new tricks and stunts. As they got older, some of the kids lost interest in biking, but Dave became more focused on it. He spent hours each day mastering old moves and learning new ones. He made friends with a few kids from elsewhere in town, and they began to ride together. Dave soon became interested in the idea of competing with others outside

BMX

BMX stands for "bicycle motocross." Back in the early 1970s, some kids in California started modifying their bicycles and riding around in vacant lots. They imitated their motorcycle heroes, trying to do similar stunts on their bicycles. A man named Bruce Brown caught much of this in his film *On Any Given Sunday*. Suddenly, it seemed that kids everywhere were modifying their bikes and riding through the dirt, not only copying motocross tricks but inventing some stunts of their own. BMX was born.

Today, BMX involves bikes with wheels with 20-inch (51 centimeter) diameters. Most BMX events can be divided into either racing or freestyle. Racing is, of course, a competition in which the riders race around a course, trying to get the best time. Freestyle (also known as bicycle stunt or trick riding) focuses on stunts and tricks and is usually performed by one rider at a time. Freestyle can be broken down into dirt jumping, flatland, park/ramp, vert, and street. Dirt jumping is the oldest form of BMX, and it involves jumping from one dirt mound and landing on another, usually performing a midair trick in between. Flatland involves riding and doing tricks on flat surfaces like parking lots. Park riding involves performing tricks on ramps and in skate parks. Vert is a specialized kind of ramp riding, using 9- to 12-foot-high (2.7- to 3.7-meter-high) ramps that end at a vertical wall. The rider rides up the ramp, performs a stunt, and then lands back on the ramp to ride back down. Street riding involves riding along the street and using whatever obstacles are found along the way, like curbs and stairs.

BMX riders often participate in more than one type of event, but most have a favorite. Dave Mirra, for example, competes in park and street, but he's best known for his vert riding.

his neighborhood and even beyond his hometown. Fortunately for him, his parents were very supportive of his interest in biking.

Dave was not big on school. His mind was busy thinking about biking most of the time, and he didn't pay much attention. That's not to say that he didn't learn anything, but he admits that, given the chance, he'd go back and focus a lot more in class. Now that he's a little older, he's a lot more interested in things like history, but as a kid, he really didn't care much about the past. He was too focused on the future. Dave did finish high school, but his grades were not stellar. Dave wasn't interested in going to college, and his chosen career didn't have much to do with schoolwork, though it did involve a lot of study.

In 1984, Dave entered his first contest, a BMX racing event in Columbus, Ohio. Dave finished a disappointing second to last. This did not stop him, however. Dave simply decided that racing was not his strong suit. He was more interested in style than in sheer speed, and he turned his focus on the freestyle element instead. He continued to ride, but now he started learning actual BMX tricks. The first two he mastered were the bunnyhop and the endo. He also switched from riding flatland (on level surfaces) to using ramps. That made a big difference, and Dave quickly became a vert fanatic. In 1987, Dave started entering BMX competitions again, this time in freestyle events. Suddenly, he was blowing away the competition.

CHAPTER TWO
THE PROFESSIONAL

In 1987, established BMX riders Ron Wilkerson, Brian Blyther, and Dave Nourie were on tour in Liverpool, New York, near Dave's hometown. All three were part of the Haro Bikes team, and they met and were impressed by a young BMX rider named Dave Mirra. The Haro team gave the teenage Dave a bike and paid for his hotel room and his meals. Dave was in heaven. He had never expected this kind of attention, and he felt that, if Haro Bikes was showing such interest in him, he must actually have potential.

Dave Mirra's aerial stunts have been captivating fans for more than a decade. Here, Dave is captured during the BMX vert finals at the 2002 X Games in Philadelphia, Pennsylvania. Mirra won the event.

Despite all that, Dave retained his amateur status for several years. He finally went professional in 1992, when he felt he was ready to make that switch. That showed a lot about Dave—many riders would have gone pro the first chance they got. Dave waited until he was sure he could handle it.

Two years later, Dave signed with Haro Bikes. It was his first major sponsor, and he has been with the company ever since, although he has added other sponsors over the years.

By the time he had graduated from high school, Dave was considered one of the best ramp riders in the world. Since then, he has proven that he deserves that title by becoming one of the most successful riders in BMX history. Dave spends three hours a day practicing in order to stay at the top of the sport. For new tricks, however, he may spend hours thinking about it before he ever tries the trick for real. The key, he says, is to visualize the trick, make sure you understand it and how to perform it, then practice it until you get it right. He also admitted that a lot of his tricks come from riding with friends, having fun, and pushing each other to do new and challenging things with the bike.

Family Ties

Dave moved to Greenville, North Carolina, in March 1995 to be closer to his older brother. The two of them started practicing together again by going to the local skate park nearly every day. Dave often credits his success to his brother and friends, saying that, without the company, he might not have practiced so often and could have lost his edge. He might have even left competition altogether.

One of the most impressive things about Dave may be his pragmatism. Some riders will do any stunt they can think of in order to make a big impression and claim they can pull off anything. Dave openly admits that some stunts scare him and that he gets nervous before every competition. He also admits that some stunts are harder than others and that it may even vary from day to day, depending on his mood and other factors. That willingness to admit limitations

Sponsoring Dave Mirra

For a professional athlete, sponsors can be crucial. This is particularly true with extreme sports. In a team sport, athletes are signed to teams and work together in return for a salary and other benefits. But athletes in individual sports don't have teams in the same way. Instead, they find companies that give them money in return for wearing that company's logo and, if appropriate, gear. Basically, the athlete serves as a representative for that company.

Dave Mirra with some of his sponsors on display

Two athletes can have the same corporate sponsor, and technically both can be on that company's "team" and yet still compete against one another. It's also possible, and even common, to have more than one sponsor at a time. Most companies insist that their athletes do not use competing products or sign with their competition. Having sponsors provides the athletes with money to pay for equipment, training facilities, and travel to competitions. The companies may also provide their own products for free.

Dave's first sponsor was a small company called General Bikes. His first major sponsor was Haro Bikes, and he has been with them for the past nine years. He has also signed with Acclaim Sports, Slim Jim, Fox Racing, Adidas, DC Shoes, Bell Helmets, Dodge, Arnette, Club Med, Famous Fixins, Troy Lee Designs, Miracle Boy, and Nyquist. Of course an athlete can also lose or change existing ones. Dave switched from Adidas to DC Shoes because he felt that DC was more interested in working with him.

and to recognize the chance of failure is rare among extreme athletes. Most try to succeed by assuming they are invincible and daring the world to prove them wrong. Dave actually thinks through every move, every stunt, and every competition, and plans what he will do and how he will execute it. He knows his own abilities, but he also recognizes his limitations and finds ways to work around them.

Famous Tricks

Every biker has preferred tricks, the ones he or she is best known for. Dave has two: the triple tailwhip and the double backflip. Here are the basics for those two tricks. (Please note: These tricks are performed by professional bike riders and should not be performed by a novice.)

Tailwhip

1. Take your right foot and move it over the top tube to the left side of your bike.

2. Jam your right foot into the area where the front tire meets the fork.

3. Swing the back of the bike around, moving your left foot off the pedal, so that the frame rotates around the front wheel.

The bunnyhop is a basic BMX stunt. The biker lifts up the front wheels, shifts his or her weight to the back of the bike, and lifts up with his or her legs. This causes the bike to rise off the ground.

4. When the bike has done a 360-degree rotation, put your left foot on the top tube and return your right foot to the pedal.

5. Put your left foot back on the pedal and land.

Backflip

1. Hit the ramp fast.

2. Pull hard on the handlebars, up and back.

3. Arch your back, lead with your head, and eye your landing spot.

4. Spin until your bike is facing front again.

5. Land on the front wheel, then the back wheel will come down. Keep your knees bent.

Keep in mind that the instructions above are for a single tailwhip and a single backflip. During a tailwhip, Dave can rotate his bike three times before landing, and he can backflip twice. Considering that both of the single versions are professional-level tricks, his versions are twice (and three times) as impressive!

The Foam Factor

One of the most recent problems for Dave has been the foam factor. More and more skate parks have foam pits now, where bikers and other athletes can practice their tricks. The foam provides a softer surface for landings, which means that the athletes don't have to worry as much about getting hurt. This also allows athletes to try newer, riskier tricks and to perfect them (or discard them) on foam before ever trying them on a regular ramp. Dave has admitted in interviews over the last few years that those athletes had an advantage over people like himself, who didn't have regular access to a foam pit. He had to practice harder to keep up with those bikers and had a greater risk of injury. But he didn't complain about it or claim that the other athletes were cheating in any way. Dave encourages everyone to use foam pits for practice, particularly beginning bikers and those trying new tricks. He built his own training facility in Greenville and included a foam pit so that he could practice more easily as well. The fact that he did not yell or scream or accuse those using foam of cheating but simply worked to gain access to similar facilities shows his maturity and his ability to adapt to the changes in his sport—the mark of a true professional.

CHAPTER THREE
MIRACLE BOY

Most extreme sports athletes have nicknames, and Dave Mirra is no exception. He is known far and wide as the Miracle Boy. Most people think he earned that name because of his amazing vert stunts. But the name has a much more serious and personal meaning.

In 1993, Dave was walking across the street when a drunk driver ran a light. The car hit him head-on, and Dave smashed face-first into the windshield and flipped over the car. Dave was lucky to survive at all, but he was even luckier to walk away with only one physical injury—a dislocated

It's all in a day's work: Dave takes a spill during the 2001 X Games in Philadelphia. Even superstars like Dave insist on wearing proper safety gear at all times.

shoulder. But the accident also left Dave with a blood clot in his brain, and doctors told him that he would never ride again. Dave proved them wrong and made a miraculous recovery. He attributes his recovery to his love of riding and the fact that he simply could not give it up.

Two years later, in 1995, Dave had another serious accident. This time it was while riding. Dave was performing a trick when his shirt got tangled in the handlebars. He lost control of the bike and fell 20 feet (6 m) to the ground. He was rushed to the hospital, where doctors had to remove

Words of Wisdom

One thing Dave always tells beginning bikers is to wear their safety gear. He himself wears a full-face helmet, elbow pads, knee pads, and gloves. It's too easy to get hurt while riding, especially if you're doing ramp riding and particularly if you're trying to learn a new trick.

Another tip is to visualize a trick before you try it. Dave uses this technique himself, making sure he understands how a trick works and what he needs to do at each step before he attempts it for real. Understanding is the first step, because if you don't know what you're doing, there's no way you can tell your body the right things to do. But if you do know, then it's easy to give yourself directions and it's just a matter of mastering them.

Dave makes a run during the bike stunt park finals at the 2002 X Games in Philadelphia.

Finally, Dave always tries to keep a positive attitude, and he encourages others to do the same. It's important to do your best, and one of the ways to manage that is to have fun and enjoy yourself. Biking is supposed to be fun, after all. If you're having a good time, you'll perform better because you're more into it. If you don't want to be there on that bike, something will be lacking, no matter how good you are.

his spleen to save his life. Once again, his ability to survive, to walk, and to ride were in doubt. Yet Dave survived, recovered, and went right back to riding again. Two miracles in a row. It's no wonder he's called the Miracle Boy!

Over the years, Dave has had several other injuries, including a fractured skull. The fact that he survived each time and never lost his skills is definitely miraculous. A lot of it, however, also has to do with his strong will. A less dedicated person might have given up after any one of those accidents, accepting the doctors' statements that his competitive career was over. Others might have tried to recover but been plagued by doubt and fear. In a competitive sport like BMX riding, that lack of confidence can cause the athlete to get sloppy and make mistakes. But Dave never gave up, and he refused to think he could not recover fully. He worked his body and mind to get back into shape after each injury, and he has proved that he has not lost anything. His injuries have only made him appreciate what he has even more and given him the determination to succeed, as evidenced by the fact that most of his major wins happened after those serious accidents. Dave has said in interviews that he never takes his health for granted. His strongest motivation is looking back at everything he has and everything riding has given him. His positive attitude after so many injuries and setbacks may be the greatest miracle of all.

Tools of the Trade

It's always important to have the right tools for the job, and extreme sports are no exception. A good biker can make do on a lesser bike, but he won't really be able to shine unless he's riding a good machine.

Dave has been fairly lucky in that respect. His first major sponsor, Haro Bikes, is one of the best BMX bike manufacturers in the world. Since Dave was on the Haro team, he had access to their bikes, which meant that he could really demonstrate his full ability. As his fame grew, Dave even got the opportunity to work with Haro and design new bikes the way he wanted them. Haro now sells four different Dave Mirra BMX bike models. And one of them, the Mirra S351 Pro, is the bike Dave himself rides in every competition.

The Mirra S351 Pro costs about $800, but bike enthusiasts say it's worth every penny. The fact that this bike has been used to win more X Games gold medals than any other bike ever only enhances the bike's reputation. The bike comes in either metal or gray and weighs about 35 pounds (16 kilograms).

The Bike

If you're in the market to buy your own bike, there are a few mechanical terms you should get to know. Bikes are surprisingly complicated, and if you're not a bike enthusiast, there's no reason you'd recognize the various terms for the different bike parts. Here are the basics, however.

bearings These contain small steel balls (ball bearings) to let the wheel move more smoothly. You can find them in the bottom bracket, in the pedals, and in the handlebars.

Dave designs the specifications for the bikes he uses during competition. Here, Dave is captured in motion on his signature bike at the 2003 T-Mobile Ramps and Amps Invitational at Randall's Island in New York City.

chainwheel Most BMX bikes have three of these. The bike chain runs across the bike's frame, connecting the pedals to the wheels, thus carrying motion from the pedals to the wheels.

crank This is attached to the frame and helps the pedals turn.

frame The basic body of the bike. BMX bikes have smaller frames than road bikes, which makes them easier to control. The vertical tube, which connects to the seat post, is also at more of an angle, providing increased comfort and smoother steering.

freewheel A freewheel is part of the pedal system and contains five, six, or seven sprockets.

gear cable This cable connects the gear lever to the chainwheel or freewheel gear system. It's covered in a plastic tube (housing).

grip Part of the handlebar that is ridged or covered to provide more traction for your hands.

nipple The nipples are tiny tubes at the beginning of the rim that hold the spokes.

rim This is the outer portion of the wheel, holding the tire itself, and is usually made of lightweight aluminum.

seat post The piece connecting the seat to the rest of the frame. It's usually adjustable, so the seat can be raised or lowered.

shocks These absorb vibrations, to make the ride smoother and to keep the rider from being bounced off the bike. They can be placed on the front or back of the bike, or both.

spoke Spokes are the thin metal rods linking the tire rim to the center of the wheel.

The BMX bike is built smaller than the typical road bike, making it easier to handle. This is especially important for riders who want to perform complex stunts.

sprocket/derailleur gear system This is the gear system used to shift the bike chain to increase or decrease tension in the pedals. This affects how much the wheels spin.

top tube This is the bar across the top of the frame of the bike that protects the rider from falling forward.

Like other extreme sports, BMX can be a challenging and risky activity. Professionals like Dave always wear full protective gear, such as a helmet and knee pads, so they can push themselves to their limits.

The bike is the most important piece of equipment, but it's far from the only one. The other key elements are clothing and safety gear. Dave takes his safety seriously and wears full safety gear, including a helmet, knee pads, and elbow pads. Dave helped design the pads, which are produced by one of his sponsors, Fox Racing. Like most BMX bikers, he also wears gloves, a racing jersey (which has built-in padding), and racing pants. Any long-sleeved shirt and pants can be worn while competing, but the racing apparel has extra padding and is made from tougher material to provide more protection. Shoes are also important, and Dave wears his own signature shoe from DC Shoes.

CHAPTER FOUR
MASTER OF X

One of the ways that an athlete proves himself or herself is by winning competitions, showcases, and other major events. In the world of extreme sports, the most important annual event is the X Games, short for Extreme Games. Every year, athletes in every extreme sport compete at these games, and this is where fans of those sports go to watch for new tricks, new stars, and current stars defending their titles.

The first X Games were held in Newport, Rhode Island, and at Mount Snow, Vermont, from June 24 to July 1, 1995.

Dave goes airborne at the 1999 X Games with the San Francisco–Oakland Bay Bridge in the background.

They were organized by ESPN as a way to showcase alternative, or extreme, sports. Nine different sports were represented, and almost 200,000 people attended. That was enough to convince ESPN to repeat the event the following year. ESPN shortened the name, however, calling it the X Games instead. The first half was held in Rhode Island again, but this time ESPN added a winter version, the Winter X Games, which were held at the Snow Summit Mountain Resort in Big Bear Lake, California, from January 30 to February 2, 1997.

Let the Games Begin

Over the years, many new extreme sports have been added to both the Summer and Winter X Games. Currently, the Summer X Games include the following sports: bicycle stunt (vert, dirt, street park, flatland, downhill), motocross (freestyle, step up, big air), bungee jumping, skysurfing, street luge (dual, mass, super mass, king of the hill), skateboarding (vert singles, vert doubles, street/park, vert best trick, street best trick), sport climbing (difficulty, speed), the x-venture race, in-line skating (combined vert, street/park, vert triples, downhill), and water sports (barefoot waterski jumping, wakeboarding).

The Winter X Games include the following: crossover, ski boarding, ice climbing (difficulty, speed), skiing (big air, skier x, super-pipe, slope style), snowboarding (big air, boarder x, half-pipe, super-pipe, slope style), super-modified shovel racing, snow mountain bike racing (downhill, speed, biker x), snowmobiling (snocross, hillcross), ultra-cross, and motocross (big air).

In 1997, the Summer X Games were moved to San Diego, California. The Winter X Games moved the following year, to Crested Butte, Colorado. Then, in 1999, the summer games moved to San Francisco, California. The events continue to move around. In 2001 and 2002, the summer games were in Philadelphia, Pennsylvania, while the winter games moved to Aspen, Colorado, in 2003. Each set of games stays in its new location for only two years.

The Summer X Games are traditionally more popular than the Winter X Games and regularly draw more than

Over the years, Dave has become a fan favorite. Here, he takes the stage at the ESPN Action Sports and Music Awards at the Universal Amphitheatre in Los Angeles in April 2002.

200,000 people each year. The Winter X Games usually get around 30,000 people, although the numbers have reached as high as 83,000. That was in 2000, when the games returned to Mount Snow, Vermont.

More recently, ESPN has added the X Trials, in which athletes qualify for the X Games, and the X Games Road Show, a two-day interactive show that travels around the country. ESPN has also created the Xperience, a promotional tour for the X Games.

The Popularity of Dave Mirra

One of the reasons Dave Mirra is such a popular biker is that he has won more awards than almost any other biker in the history of BMX competition. He also holds the record for the most gold medals ever won at the X Games, with a total of ten (he has also won three silver medals, for a grand total of thirteen X Game medals). He has won in both vert and street competitions. Every year, BMX freestyle fans flock to the X Games to see what he will do next and to see whether he can hold on to the title. In 2001, for example, he performed the first-ever double backflip in competition. In 2002, he impressed fans and judges alike with his double tailwhips.

Dave acknowledges that the X Games put a lot of pressure on competitors. A lot of people are watching them, and there are always new athletes with new tricks that no one has ever seen before. He also admits that things don't always go as planned at these competitions. A trick that worked perfectly in practice could wind up failing at the show for a variety of reasons. In interviews, he has explained that the key is to relax and do your best, but to try and enjoy it. Don't worry about following your planned program precisely. Instead, he says, remember that you love this sport and be comfortable with yourself and with

ESPN's X Games have helped propel extreme sports into the national spotlight. The X Games are also a venue for top athletes to inspire and challenge each other. Inset: Competitors Dave *(left)*, Mat Hoffman *(middle)*, and Simon Tabron *(right)* look on during competition at the 2002 ESPN X Games in Philadelphia.

what you can do. That's the secret to giving your best possible performance. Judging from all those medals, Dave knows what he's talking about!

There is no doubt that Dave Mirra is one of the best BMX bikers in the world, but he's not the only one out there. There is a long list of excellent athletes in the sport, and several other athletes today are biking at Dave's level. Dave says this is a good thing because it keeps him on his toes. Having people of that caliber around just means that he pushes himself harder and that all of them push the limits of the sport every day.

Other Gamers

Here are a few other great BMX bikers to watch for at events and in the news.

Chad Degroot Chad was born on March 23, 1974, in Green Bay, Wisconsin. His specialty is flatland riding, and in 2002, he won the Number One Rider Award (NORA) Cup and became Flatland Rider of the Year. He is also the first flatland rider to become a video game character and was pleased to help increase the popularity of flatland riding.

Mat Hoffman Born in Oklahoma City, Oklahoma, on January 9, 1972, Mat has been biking since 1982 and competing since 1984. He's considered one of the first stars of BMX, and he certainly has the medals to prove it. Mat won the BMX World Championship in vert a record ten times! He also invented many of the bike stunts other riders like Dave Mirra later perfected. He starred in the first BMX computer game, which led to later projects, such as Dave Mirra Freestyle BMX. Mat's nickname is the Condor.

Dennis McCoy Born on December 29, 1966, in Kansas City, Missouri, Dennis is one of the oldest BMX bikers still competing today. He has been competing since 1985 but has actually been riding bikes since he was four. DMC, as Dennis is called, is also the head of McCoy Productions, which runs the bike stunt portion of the Vans Triple Crown Series and the Gravity Games.

Ryan Nyquist Although he has been competing only since 1995, Ryan is already considered one of the best of the new BMX bikers. Born on March 6, 1979, in Los Gatos, California, Ryan has won a total of eight X Game medals. He's also one of the most versatile riders in BMX—his medals are in dirt, street, park, and vert. He lives in Greenville, North Carolina, the same town Dave Mirra calls home.

Jamie Staff Born on April 30, 1973, in Ashford, Great Britain, Jamie now lives in California. He has been competing since 1983, the same year he learned to ride. Since then, Jamie has won several medals, and he is considered one of the best riders by both the American Bike Association (ABA) and the National Biking League (NBL), two major organizations that helped turn BMX into an organized and competitive sport. Jamie and Dave are friends and watch each other's runs closely in competitions.

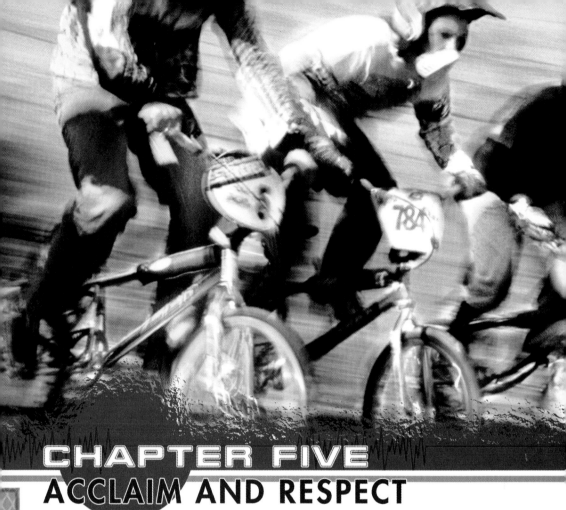

CHAPTER FIVE
ACCLAIM AND RESPECT

Toward the end of the twentieth century, BMX was recognized as an extreme sport by enthusiasts. It had its own competitions and its own celebrities. But most people who didn't ride had never heard of the sport or the athletes involved.

That all changed when Acclaim, a video game company, released its first extreme sports game: Dave Mirra Freestyle BMX. This game, which appeared for both Sega Dreamcast and Sony PlayStation platforms, was the first to involve real athletes in the creation process. Dave helped

Video games like Dave Mirra Freestyle BMX have increased the popularity of the sport.

come up with the list of tricks and trick names. But more than that, he put on a motion-capture suit and spent more than eight hours performing stunts so that the game could be more realistic and accurate.

The game offered more trick options for players, and it didn't hurt that one of BMX's biggest stars had his name on the cover. The game sold tremendously well and was a huge success with fans. A second game, Dave Mirra Freestyle BMX2, came out a year later and was also successful. By April 2002, the two games together had sold more than 3 million copies worldwide, and Acclaim had signed Dave to an exclusive five-year contract.

Controversy

Later that year, however, things suddenly changed. Acclaim announced that it would be producing not one but two BMX games. Dave Mirra 3 would still come out but later than expected. It had been moved back on the schedule to make room for Acclaim's new BMX game, called BMX XXX. This newer title featured more mature content, including crude humor and nudity. Acclaim had shown off the new game at E3 (the annual major show for video games, held in California) earlier that year and had shocked most of the viewers, particularly with the game's use of nudity. The game was released in November 2002 but did not do as well as the first two Mirra titles, in part because it was banned by several major stores (including Wal-Mart, Kmart, and Toys "R" Us).

But apparently that wasn't enough for Dave. In February 2003, he filed a lawsuit against Acclaim. Dave claimed that, back in March 2002, he and Acclaim had discussed the new game, and at the time, it had been described as a more playful, tongue-in-cheek game, not the rude version that appeared on store shelves around the country. Dave was all in favor of the original version, but Acclaim later changed the game's focus, making it much more adult in content. That was when Dave objected. Acclaim agreed to remove his name from the title, which is why they renamed it BMX XXX. But in his lawsuit, Dave claimed that Acclaim had still used his name and likeness

It's Gotta Be the Shoes

Star athletes are often asked to endorse various products they use for their sport. Tennis players, for example, endorse rackets, clothing, and headbands. Bikers usually endorse bikes, sunglasses, and gloves. But one thing almost any athlete can endorse is shoes because most sports require not just footwear but very specialized footwear.

Dave Mirra was approached a few years ago by DC Shoes with the idea of endorsing a shoe for BMX riding. Dave liked the idea but wanted a more hands-on approach if he was going to put his name on the product. The result was the Dave Mirra signature shoe. Designed specifically for BMX riders or skateboarders, the shoe has a sturdy upper layer with flexible toe caps for added protection. The heel has extra reinforcements. Mesh panels keep the foot cool and comfortable, and a soft lining provides extra comfort, while elastic tongue straps give more stability and support. The midsole is lightweight polyurethane, but the outsole has a sticky gum-rubber bottom for better traction. The shoe also has a heel strap and a shock-absorbing heel airbag to disperse impact. Some of these features were already available in skateboarding shoes, but the sole and other aspects were added by the designers to make the shoes even more functional.

In the fall of 2002, DC released an updated version of the shoe, with even more features. It had a sock liner, so that the shoe would stay secure even if the biker preferred to leave the laces loose, and it was even more flexible in front to allow better control of the pedals. Dave was heavily involved in the design of both versions and was very happy with the results. Bikers everywhere also seem pretty happy with them, too. It's just another way that Dave has made his mark on the sport.

in the game itself and that this could injure his reputation. He demanded $21 million in damages.

Some of the fans were upset over this, saying that Dave was only suing Acclaim for the money. Others suggested that, with BMX XXX's poor sales, Dave might be worried that Acclaim would cancel plans for Mirra 3, and with several years remaining on his contract with Acclaim, he couldn't go to another software company until that time was up. But if Acclaim canceled its contract because of the lawsuit, Dave would be free to appear in games by other companies.

Dave himself stated that his only reason for suing Acclaim was anger over the company's misuse of him and his image. He told fans that he had taken his name off the game because he felt it would not be appropriate for younger fans, and he didn't want to be associated with that. Acclaim stated in a press release that Dave's lawsuit had no basis in fact and that the company would fight it in court.

In October 2003, the case was finally settled. Dave was not awarded any money from the suit and will remain under contract with Acclaim until 2011. This is great news for fans. Perhaps with this behind them, both parties can move on and produce new Dave Mirra games that have the quality of the first two installments.

Recognition

In the ten years since he turned pro, Dave Mirra has certainly won a lot of competitions. But he has also won other awards and opportunities. It is these, as much as his medals, that have made him almost a household name and arguably the most famous BMX biker of all time.

BMX heroes like Dave continue to inspire future generations of riders. Here, Dave signs an autograph for an enthusiastic fan during a break at the T-Mobile Ramps and Amps Invitational held at Randall's Island in New York City in July 2003.

In 2000, Dave's name and likeness began appearing on shoes, bikes, and other merchandise. He was one of the few alternative sports athletes to gain widespread media exposure and to be recognized as a sports icon by non-bikers and non-extreme sports enthusiasts.

In 2001, Dave was voted BMX Rider of the Year at the first ESPN Action Sports and Music Awards. He had been voted Freestyler of the Year by *BMX Magazine* in 1999, but

that award had been noticed only by BMX fans, whereas the ESPN awards were more widely publicized. He has also appeared on the cover of *Sports Illustrated for Kids* and has been featured in *Rolling Stone* and *ESPN Magazine*. Dave has also made several television appearances on shows such as *Good Morning America*, Disney's *The Jersey Show*, and *The Late Show with David Letterman*. All of this has combined to make him one of the most recognized extreme sports athletes in the world (probably second behind skateboarder Tony Hawk).

Dave has even appeared on the big screen. He was featured in ESPN's motion picture *Ultimate X*, which reached theaters in May 2002 and brought extreme sports to a new audience.

While reaching new people is important, Dave has not forgotten his existing fans. He often takes time to participate in online chats and has done several major tours, both his own (the Dave Mirra Tour) and others' (like the Tony Hawk Tour and the Huckjam tour). Dave has kept very active over the last few years, and part of that activity has involved keeping in touch with people and staying visible. Everyone gets older, and at some point, Dave will most likely hang up his gear and quit competing, but that will not prevent people from recognizing him or from

Dave backflips his bike into a 4,000-gallon (15 kiloliter) vat of green slime at the 15th Annual Nickelodeon Kids' Choice Awards at the Barker Hangar in Santa Monica, California, in April 2002.

Dave Mirra: Career highlights

Dave holds more X Game gold medals—thirteen in all—than any other X Games competitor. He has taken the gold in the following events:

2003 Global X Games — park

2002 Summer X Games — vert

2001 Summer X Games — vert

2000 Summer X Games — park

1999 Summer X Games — street and vert

1998 Summer X Games — street, vert, and vert doubles

1997 Summer X Games — street and vert

1996 Summer X Games — street and vert

He has also taken three silvers at the X Games:

2000 Summer X Games — vert

1996 Summer X Games — vert

1995 Summer X Games — vert

Dave also took gold medals in both park and vert at the 2003 Nokia FISE in Montpellier, France. He won a gold in park and a silver in vert at the 2002 Gravity Games, a silver in park at the 2003 Vans Triple Crown of BMX, and a silver in vert at the 2002 EXPN Invitational. He also took the gold in park at the 2002 UGP Roots Jam in Orlando, Florida; gold in both park and vert at the 2001 B3 event in Anaheim, California; and a gold in park at the 2001 B3 event in Louisville, Kentucky. That year he also got a silver in street at the 2001 Vans Triple Crown of BMX.

remembering him as one of BMX's greatest stars. Dave loves what he does, and that shows in every interview and appearance. His enthusiasm is infectious, and the fans love to watch him perform. They also love to see him and meet him and ask him questions. And more and more people outside the sport have begun to recognize and admire him as well.

CHAPTER SIX
TODAY AND BEYOND

The last few years have been busy ones for Dave Mirra, both in biking and otherwise. In 2002, while competing at the Vans Triple Crown in Charlotte, North Carolina, he injured his elbow. The wound required stitches, and unfortunately it got infected. Dave wound up spending two nights in the hospital and having surgery to repair the damage. He spent the next several months recovering and healing. But that doesn't mean he was idle. While his elbow was healing, he went up to New York to visit his family and to ride in an OzFest parade, celebrating

Today, Dave Mirra continues to be one of the biggest names in all extreme sports. Here, Dave performs a trick in the street bike finals at the 2002 Gravity Games in Cleveland. He placed first in the event.

L. Frank Baum, the man who wrote *The Wizard of Oz* (and who was born near Dave's hometown). A few months later, Dave was back at the Gravity Games. He won a gold medal in park and a silver in vert.

Dave is an avid golfer, and Greenville is known for its golf courses (former basketball star Michael Jordan holds his charity golf events in the same city). In the summer of 2001, Dave started a golf event of his own, the Dave Mirra Charity Golf Tournament. All of the proceeds went to the American Cancer Society. The tournament has become an

annual event, and each year the money goes to another charity, like the Dream Factory, a children's charity. When asked where he sees himself in five or ten years, Dave has even said that he could be in the PGA (Professional Golf Association). He might be joking, but he does love golf, and if he takes that hobby as seriously as he does BMX, and practices as hard, Dave just might wind up becoming a winning athlete in that sport as well.

The Future of BMX

When asked about the future of BMX, Dave admits that he doesn't know where the sport will go over the next few years. It could become more technical, with athletes concentrating on more precise tricks. Or it could simply get grander, with bigger airs and bigger, more elaborate tricks. He has mentioned before that more people get into street riding than into vert because vert is harder to learn, harder to master, and more dangerous for the athlete. But he does feel that new people are entering the sport all the time and that the sport continues to grow. Part of that, of course, is that BMX is becoming more familiar to more people. Kids can play the video games now, which means they know about BMX riding even if they've never tried it themselves. Plus, people can watch

The Philly Phanatic (*left*), Dave (*middle*), and Jason Michaels (*right*) of the Philadelphia Phillies meet during a game break on August 13, 2002. Being a top extreme athlete involves a lot of hard work, but it also offers many fun rewards.

BMX events on television. And athletes are always trying new tricks, both to improve their own skills and to overwhelm the competition. According to Dave, as long as people continue to be creative and have fun with vert, it will continue to grow. And that's the most important thing. Everyone involved should enjoy themselves and love what they do.

Another project Dave started in 2001 was the Dave Mirra BMX Super Tour, a traveling exhibition of BMX biking. Dave and his friends stopped in various U.S. cities (twelve in all) and performed for crowds as a way to get more people interested in the sport. It was also a chance for fans to see Dave and his friends do their tricks and for younger bikers to meet the pros and perhaps get a few pointers. Both ESPN and ESPN2 covered the tour, which meant that even more people became familiar with BMX in general and with Dave in particular.

Dave has also taken part in other tours. He has participated in the Tony Hawk Tour, which gathers some of the top athletes from several different extreme sports, including skateboarding and biking. And in 2003, he took part in Tony Hawk's Boom Boom HuckJam. This was a newer, larger, more elaborate tour that Tony Hawk organized, and he enlisted the help of some of extreme sports' best, including Dave and Mat Hoffman (BMX); Cary Hart and Ronnie Faist (motorcycle); and Shaun White and Bob Burnquist (skateboarding). Recently, Dave talked with EXPN.com about performing with the tour: "[It] was kind of like the old days when we all did shows together . . . It just made you want to give 110 percent and throw out the best tricks you could."

During the 2002 Tony Hawk Boom Boom HuckJam in Anaheim, California, Dave Mirra grabs air above the halfpipe, while pulling off a no-footed can-can.

The tour included not only these athletes performing together but also music and other activities, putting on a full show for the crowd. Mirra later told interviewers that this was the future of sports demos—not just an athlete or two, or a single sport, but an entire entertainment spectacle with several sports brought together.

Another new thing in 2003 was the Dave Mirra BMX Training Clinic, which started in August in his warehouse

in Greenville and is open to the public on Saturdays and Sundays. Whenever Dave is in town for the weekend, he's at the clinic. When he can't be there himself, other BMX pros are around to help teach the kids. These include both local pros and some of Dave's friends who come into town. It's just another way that Dave has found to give back to the community and to the sport, by providing a safe, clean place for kids to bike. He gives them tips not only on how to perform better tricks but also on how to have more fun.

Of course, while Dave's facility in Greenville is excellent, there is still a better one. That's the Woodward training camp in Pennsylvania, which most extreme athletes say is the best training space in the world. Dave himself used to go there to practice occasionally, especially before his Greenville space was finished. (Woodward was one of the first locations to get foam pits, which let athletes try out riskier ramp tricks without hurting themselves.) Now Dave has his own space, but he has recently started a Woodward Scholarship, which sends six kids to Woodward for a week. That way, some promising young athletes get the chance to train and practice at a state-of-the-art facility and hopefully learn some skills and tricks they can take back with them.

Dave Mirra eyes the ramp during the bike stunt park finals at the X Games in Los Angeles on August 16, 2003. In addition to his personal achievements in BMX, Dave works to provide kids with opportunities to experience the sport themselves.

Biographical Timeline

1974 David Michael Mirra is born on April 4 in Syracuse, New York.

1979 Starts learning biking tricks.

1984 Enters his first competition, a BMX race.

1987 Enters his first BMX freestyle competition.

1992 Turns professional.

1993 Hit by a drunk driver; damages his shoulder and has a blood clot in his brain.

1995 Gets injured while biking and has his spleen removed.

1996 Wins his first gold medals at the X Games.

1997 Again takes gold in vert and street at the X Games.

1998 Wins gold in street, vert, and vert doubles at the X Games.

1999 Wins gold in street and vert at the X Games. Voted Freestyler of the Year by *BMX Magazine*.

2000 Wins gold in park and silver in vert at the X Games. Dave Mirra Freestyle BMX game is released.

2001 Is voted BMX Rider of the Year at the ESPN Action Sports and Music Awards.

2002 Wins gold in vert at the X Games. Injures his elbow, undergoes surgery.

2003 Wins gold in park at the Global X Games.

Dave has also been heavily involved with the Make-A-Wish foundation for several years. All told, he spends a lot of his time giving back to other people and trying to use his fame and his money to make a difference. That's just another reason why he's considered one of the greatest of the BMX riders and one of the best athletes in extreme sports today.

blood clot Blockage of blood in an artery or vein.

BMX The sport of riding bicycles over rough terrain and performing tricks; originally known as bicycle motocross.

caliber Degree of excellence or quality.

flatland A type of freestyle BMX riding that uses flat surfaces, like parking lots.

freestyle Also known as bicycle stunt riding or trick riding, this type of BMX riding focuses on stunts and tricks rather than on speed or racing.

park Another name for ramp riding.

pragmatism A practical, realistic approach.

ramp A type of freestyle BMX that uses ramps, usually in skate parks, to perform tricks.

spleen An organ located near the stomach; responsible for destruction of red blood cells.

street A type of freestyle BMX done on the street, using found obstacles like stairs and curbs.

vert A specialized form of ramp riding in which the ramp has a vertical wall at the top.

wheelies Bicycle stunts in which the front wheel is raised while balancing on the rear wheel.

Organizations

Adventure Cycling Association
150 East Pine Street
P.O. Box 8308
Missoula, MT 59807
(800) 755-2453

Atlantic Canada Cycling
P.O. Box 1555
Station Central, Halifax, NS B3J 2Y3
Canada
(902) 423-2453
e-mail: cycling@atl-canadacycling.com

National Off-Road Bicycling Association (NORBA)
One Olympic Plaza
Colorado Springs, CO 80909
(719) 578-4581

Web Sites

Due to the changing nature of Internet links, the Rosen Publishing Group, Inc., has developed an online list of Web sites related to the subject of this book. This site is updated regularly. Please use this link to access the list:

http://www.rosenlinks.com/exb/dmir

FOR FURTHER READING

Brimner, Larry. *BMX Freestyle* (First Books). New York: Franklin Watts, 1987.

Herran, Joe Ron Thomas, and Latty Lee Goodwin. *BMX Riding* (Action Sports). Broomall, PA: Chelsea House, 2002.

Mirra, Dave. *Mirra Images*. New York: Regan, 2003.

Nelson, Julie. *BMX Racing and Freestyle* (Extreme Sports). New York: Raintree/Steck-Vaughn, 2002.

Partland, J. P. *The World of BMX*. Chicago: Motorbooks International, 2003.

BIBLIOGRAPHY

Carlance, Chris. Interview with Dave Mirra. Retrieved September 5, 2003 (http://www.woodwardcamp.com/PIBUD/Davemirrainterview.html).

Dave Mirra interview. Haro Bicycles. Retrieved August 21, 2003 (http://www.harobikes.com/2002/inational/mirralumpur.html).

EXPN.com. Dave Mirra. Retrieved January 20, 2004 (http://expn.go.com/athletes/bios/MIRRA_DAVE.html).

Haro Bicycles. Retrieved September 3, 2003 (http://www.harobikes.com).

Hoffman Sports Association. Interview with Dave Mirra. Retrieved September 2, 2003 (http://www.hsacentral.com/old/article.cfm?pickit = 137).

ign.com. "Dave Mirra Sues Acclaim." Retrieved August 20, 2003 (http://ps2.ign.com/articles/386/386324p1.html).

InfoPlease.com. Retrieved August 24, 2003 (http://www.infoplease.com/ipsa/A0764684.html).

Losey, Mark. "Games Vert Finals." Tuesday August 22, 2003 (http://www.bmxonline.com/bmx/features/article/0,15737,476868,00.html).

McCassy, Malcolm. "The Huckjam Tour." Retreived September 15, 2002 (http://expn.go.com/bmx/mirra/s/020426_huckjam.html).

Rodriguez, Joel James. "Rider Profile: Dave 'The Miracle Boy' Mirra." Retrieved August 1, 2003 (http://www.freshangles.com/thezone/extreme/articles/18.html).

INDEX

About the Author

Aaron Rosenberg writes educational books, novels, and role-playing games, and he owns his own games company, Clockworks (http://www.clockworks.com). He grew up in New Orleans but now lives in New York.

Photo Credits

Front cover (left), pp. 15, 22, 28 (inset), 33, 35 (inset), 53 © Tony Donaldson/Icon Sports Media; front cover (right) © Duomo/Corbis; back cover © Nelson Sá; pp. 1, 25, 43, 44 © Hulton Archive/Getty Images; pp. 4, 20–21, 50 © Icon Sports Media; p. 6 © Hulton-Deutsch Collection/Corbis; pp. 8–9 © Neal Preston/Corbis; pp. 12–13 © Steve Boyle/Corbis; pp. 17, 27, 28 © Tony Donaldson/Icon Sports Media/Rosen Publishing; pp. 30–31 © Paul Sakuma/AP/World Wide Photos; p. 35 © H. Rumoh, Jr./AP/World Wide Photos; pp. 38–39 © Lester Lefkowitz/Corbis; pp. 48–49 © Al Fuchs/Corbis; p. 54 © Kohjiro Kinno/Corbis.

Designer: Nelson Sá; **Editor:** Charles Hofer; **Photo Researcher:** Peter Tomlinson